New York
History

Mark Stewart

Heinemann Library
Chicago, Illinois

Designed by Heinemann Library
Printed and bound by Lake Book Manufacturing

07 06 05 04 03
10 9 8 7 6 5 4 3 2 1

**Library of Congress Cataloging-in-
Publication Data**
Stewart, Mark, 1960-
  New York history : New York state studies / Mark
Stewart.
      p. cm.
Summary: Provides a comprehensive look at
New York state history, from the Algonquian and
Iroquois who lived there before the arrival of
Europeans to the beginning of the new millennium.
Includes bibliographical references and index.
  ISBN 1-4034-0353-8 (HC), 1-4034-0575-1 (pbk.)
  1. New York (State)--History--Juvenile literature.
[1. New York
(State)--History.] I. Title.
  F119.3.S75 2003

                                    2002154309

Acknowledgments
The author and publishers are grateful to the
following for permission to reproduce copyright
material:

Cover photographs by (top, L-R) The Granger
Collection, New York, Bettmann/Corbis, The
Granger Collection, New York, The Granger
Collection, New York; (main) The Granger
Collection, New York

Title page (L-R) Bettmann/Corbis, The Granger
Collection, New York, Corbis; contents page (L-R)
Corbis, The Granger Collection, New York; pp. 4,
5, 7, 9, 10, 12, 14, 15, 18, 19T, 20, 21, 23, 24,
26, 27B, 28, 29, 35, 40B The Granger Collection,
New York; pp. 6, 11, 30B, 33T, 39, 40T, 42
Bettmann/Corbis; pp. 8, 22, 25, 38, 44 maps.com/
Heinemann Library; pp. 13, 17, 30T, 32, 36, 37
Corbis; p. 16 Culver Pictures; pp. 19B, 27T, 33B,
34, 41 Stock Montage; p. 31 Underwood &
Underwood/Corbis; p. 43T Chris Collins/Corbis;
p. 43B Imaginary Studio, New York

Photo research by Susana Darwin

Special thanks to expert reader Edward H.
Knoblauch. Knoblauch has an MA from Syracuse
University in American History, is the webmaster
for New York History Net (www.nyhistory.com),
and was the managing editor of the Encyclopedia
of New York State.

Every effort has been made to contact copyright
holders of any material reproduced in this book.
Any omissions will be rectified in subsequent
printings if notice is given to the publisher.

Some words are shown in bold, **like this.**
You can find out what they mean by looking
in the glossary.

Contents

Three Worlds Meet: Prehistory to 1609

Each state in the United States has a story to tell about its land and people. The geography and people of New York state have defined its history. For centuries, its size, shape, **resources,** and location have attracted people from all over the world. Through war and peace, **poverty** and **prosperity,** good times and bad, New York has always been one of the most interesting states in this country.

PREHISTORIC PEOPLES

The first humans to live in the area we know today as New York arrived around 11,000 years ago. We know very little about these people because they did not leave many **artifacts** behind. **Archaeologists** are working to learn more about them. These people hunted, fished, and gathered

Below is an illustration of Native American longhouses on Manhattan Island, before it was settled by the Dutch in the 1600s.

plants for food. They honored their dead and traded with their neighbors. Toward the end of their stay in New York, they began growing corn and other crops. These first people of New York were long gone when the first Europeans settled the area in the early 1600s. The nations the Europeans did encounter at that time—the Haudenosaunee, also called Iroquois, and Algonquins—knew nothing of those who had lived there before them.

These Haudenosaunee women are shown grinding corn, an important part of their diet.

THE ALGONQUIN AND HAUDENOSAUNEE

The Algonquin people lived in what is now the southern area of New York state, on Long Island, and along the Hudson River. The Algonquin tribes included the Delaware, Mohicans, Munsee, and Wappingers. The Algonquins were skillful in using their environment. They hunted, trapped, fished, and gathered fruits, nuts, and **shellfish.**

The Haudenosaunee were very well organized. In fact, parts of today's United States government may have been inspired by the **confederation** the Haudenosaunee created in the 1500s. This confederation was called the Iroquois League. The five nations that made up the Iroquois League were the Mohawk, Oneida, Onondaga,

What's in a Name?

The word *Iroquois* is often used when referring to the people who are a part of the six New York nations. It is possible that *Iroquois* comes from the Algonquian language and means "snake." The term *Haudenosaunee* is preferred by the people of the six nations, and means "people of the longhouse."

Cayuga, and Seneca. In the early 1700s, a sixth nation, the Tuscarora, joined. The league made laws and settled arguments in peaceful ways. However, the Haudenosaunee were also skilled at making war. For much of the time that Algonquins and Haudenosaunee shared the land, which spread east to west from present-day Albany to Buffalo, the Algonquin Nation lived in fear of its northern neighbors.

Smallpox and measles, brought to the area by European settlers in the 1600s, were deadly for the Algonquins. They had no **immunity** to these diseases. Thousands of Algonquins who interacted with the settlers died from these diseases, which meant that there were few left to defend their lands.

The Haudenosaunee, who did not have as much contact with the Europeans because they lived farther inland, were not exposed to disease as the Algonquins were. Their knowledge of the land and their trapping skills made them excellent trading partners. The Haudenosaunee were also skilled farmers. Dutch and English settlers respected them because they were well organized and good warriors. The Haudenosaunee way of life was not destroyed until the American Revolution (1775–1783).

EUROPEAN CONTACT: 1500s

Although stories of **Viking** ships reaching North America more than 1,000 years ago are true, there is no evidence that they landed in New York. Starting in the early 1500s, European ships sometimes anchored off the Atlantic coast and sailors

The Italian explorer Giovanni da Verrazano first came to the coast of New York in 1524.

Samuel de Champlain (right) was one of the first Europeans in New York. Along with a group of Huron warriors, he defeated a group of Haudenosaunee on July 29, 1609.

rowed ashore. They may have landed on Long Island. We do know for a fact that in 1524, Giovanni da Verrazano, an Italian explorer, sailed his boat *La Dauphine* into what is today called New York Harbor. He left after a short time and continued his journey north along the coast.

The first European to spend a lot of time in New York was Samuel de Champlain. Champlain, a Frenchman, had spent many years trying to find a northern passage to Asia to make trading easier and faster. He thought this route might start at the St. Lawrence River, which runs between Canada and northern New York state. Champlain thought that the people of the Huron Nation of Ontario, Canada, knew the answer to this mystery. In hopes of gaining their help, he agreed to help the Huron fight their enemy to the south, the Haudenosaunee of New York. In 1609, Champlain led a band of 60 Huron warriors into New York. They defeated 200 Haudenosaunee near what later was called Lake Champlain, named for Samuel de Champlain.

Colonization and Settlement: 1609–1763

Henry Hudson, an English **navigator** working for the Dutch, also explored New York in 1609. He started in the south and made his way north. He, too, was searching for a shortcut to Asia. Hudson believed that there was

When Europeans arrived in New York in the 1500s, there were two main groups of Native American Indians: the Algonquin and the Haudenosaunee.

Native American Nations at the Time of European Contact

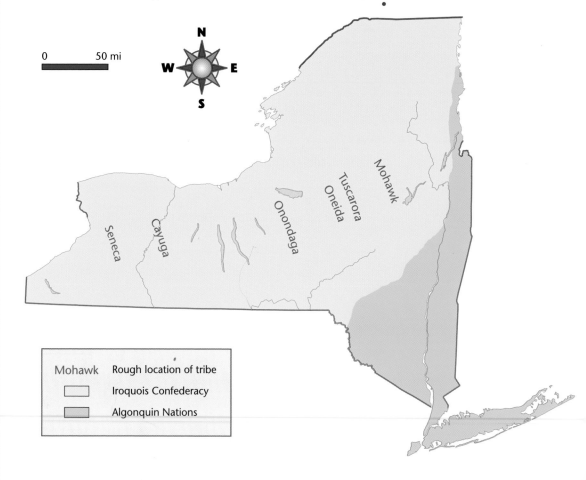

0   50 mi

N
W   E
S

Seneca
Cayuga
Onondaga
Oneida
Tuscarora
Mohawk

Mohawk   Rough location of tribe

Iroquois Confederacy

Algonquin Nations

an ice-free stretch of sea at the North Pole, and he set out to discover it. When Hudson's ship, the *Half Moon,* ran into dangerous ice in the Atlantic Ocean, his crew refused to continue. Hudson did not want to return to Europe without something to show for his voyage, so he changed direction and began to look for a way to get to China along the North American coast.

Hudson explored the Delaware Bay before sailing into a river he hoped would lead to the Pacific Ocean. Late in the summer of 1609, Hudson sailed into New York Harbor. He turned north and continued for about 175 miles on the Hudson River. When the river got too shallow near Albany, the *Half Moon* had to turn back. Hudson claimed all of the land he encountered for the Dutch.

NEW NETHERLAND: 1614

In 1614, after hearing Hudson's reports of the New World, Dutch traders arrived in New York. They built a fur-trading post—Fort Nassau—on the banks of the Hudson River, near present-day Albany. Hudson had reported that the area was beautiful and the riches plentiful. New Netherland, as the site was called, became the first permanent European settlement in the state. Approximately 25 to 30 families came to live in New Netherland. In 1626, the Dutch built a second settlement, called New Amsterdam, on the tip of Manhattan Island. In exchange for the land, the Dutch leader Peter Minuit traded the local Algonquins 60 **guilders** worth

Peter Minuit is shown here purchasing the island of Manhattan from the Algonquin Nation in 1626.

*This is the earliest known image of the settlement of New Amsterdam as it looked in 1626. This **engraving** was made in 1651.*

t' Fort nieúw Amſterdam op de Manhatans

of goods, which is estimated to be about 24 dollars. Minuit also bought Staten Island. Manhattan was renamed New Amsterdam, and a small fort was built. It is likely that the Algonquin people did not have the same beliefs about owning land as the Dutch, and were not aware that the Dutch felt the land belonged entirely to them.

Life in New Netherland was different from other colonies for two important reasons. First, it was the only colony in North America founded by the Dutch. The Dutch were the most successful traders in the world at that time. They brought this spirit with them to New Netherland. The primary goal of the Dutch settlers was to make money. They did not have long-term plans to settle more and more land in the New World.

New Amsterdam

Although New Amsterdam's population grew to 2,000 under Dutch rule, it was never really a city. It was little more than a seaport—ships came in, loaded up, and sailed away. The Dutch did not want to get involved in the lives of the people who lived there. They thought of New Amsterdam as a money-making experiment: the less contact they had with the American Indians, the more money they would make.

Second, New Netherland was different from colonies that had been established based on religious ideals. Although Dutch settlers attended church, they were not governed by religious leaders as were the early French, Spanish, and English settlers of New England. When Peter Stuyvesant became New Amsterdam's leader in 1647, he was shocked at how wild the colony had become. In an effort to make things better, he closed the **taverns** on Sunday, discouraged the ball games that often interrupted the workday, and passed laws to make people take better care of their homes and businesses.

ENGLISH CONTROL: 1664

The English, unlike the French, wanted the farmland in the southern part of the state. They wanted to settle the land. In 1664, four English warships captured the Dutch fort in New Amsterdam without a fight. It became the property of Charles II, the king of England, who then gave it to his brother, the Duke of York and Albany. New Netherland was renamed New York. The English allowed the Dutch settlers to stay, and in some places the Dutch language was still being spoken 250 years later.

Homes built by the Dutch settlers in New York often resembled the types of homes that they had in The Netherlands.

THE POPULATION GROWS: 1650–1750

The English made treaties with the Haudenosaunee and Algonquin Nations. Because of these treaties, English settlers were able to spread north and west

*This **engraving** shows New York's American Indians trading furs with European fur traders.*

from Manhattan and out from the shores of the Hudson River. No matter where people lived, however, life at that time was a struggle for survival.

On the eastern shore of the Hudson River, the Dutch and the English gave large land grants to people who would rent the land to poor farmers. This was to encourage settlement of the area. In the northern part of the colony, around Albany, wealthy Dutch **patroons** owned much of the land. Poorer families farmed the land for the owners, who collected a share of what the families grew as rent. Along New York's western **frontier,** pioneer families hunted, trapped, and farmed among the Haudenosaunee.

In New York City, most people worked with their hands—hauling, building, cleaning, and creating. There were a few skilled craftsmen who worked for the city's growing **upper class,** but people usually found work doing physical labor. Life was hard and often dangerous.

New York was an English city in an English colony, but many languages, from Dutch to Portuguese, were spoken by its residents.

THE FRENCH AND INDIAN WAR: 1754–1763

Great Britain and France continued to fight for control of New York. By the mid-1700s, the British in North America outnumbered the French by at least ten British people to one French person. This worried the French. They knew it would only be a matter of time before English settlers pushed west to the Mississippi River.

From June 19, 1754, to July 11, 1754, representatives from the colonies of New York, Pennsylvania, Maryland, Massachusetts, Connecticut, Rhode Island, and New Hampshire met in Albany, New York. Their meeting was called the Albany Congress. The representatives knew that a war was likely to break out between Britain and France in North America, and they met to decide what to do about it. The representatives invited leaders from the Six Nations of the Haudenosaunee, and a treaty was made. The Haudenosaunee agreed to fight with the British should a war break out with the French.

The French began to build forts and send soldiers along the Mississippi River in

This drawing by Benjamin Franklin was first published on May 9, 1754. The different sections of the snake represent the different British colonies. Franklin's point was that if the colonies did not come together and support one another, they would not be able to win a war against the French and American Indians.

anticipation of the war. In 1754, fighting broke out along the **frontier** between the French and British settlers. That was the start of the French and Indian War.

Because of New York's many waterways and its common border with French-held Canada, the state was the site of many battles. The British were able to defeat the French at Fort Carillon, Crown Point, and Fort Niagara, but not without the help of the Haudenosaunee. The Haudenosaunee were good fighters and excellent scouts. Also, the Haudenosaunee were enemies of the nations that chose to fight with the French, including the Algonquins. When the war ended in 1763, only a small part of North America remained under French control.

••

*This **engraving** shows the Battle of Lake George in 1755. The British defeated the French, strengthening their claim to the region.*

Revolution and the New Nation: 1776–1860

New York had existed as a British colony for over 100 years when on July 9, 1776, it became one of the first thirteen states of what would become the United States. A new state **constitution** was written and adopted on April 20, 1777. George Clinton became New York's first **governor.**

FIGHTING IN NEW YORK

Despite the colonists' declaration of independence, Britain refused to give up its hold. New York, because of its location and the importance of many of its cities, played a vital role in the American Revolution. About one of every three battles of the Revolution was fought there. In 1776, the British set out to capture the land between New York City and Montreal, Canada. One of the first major battles of the war was fought on Long Island.

One reason colonists wanted to govern themselves is they felt the British were taxing them unfairly. In this image, colonists have strung up a British tax agent.

American Flag

The first time in history that an "American" flag was flown over a fort was in the summer of 1777. Continental soldiers at Fort Stanwix in Rome, New York, fought off a large force of British **redcoats** and their **allies,** the Haudenosaunee. The flag was created from bits and pieces of material collected from around the fort, and featured red and blue stripes, but no stars.

As commander of the **Continental Army,** George Washington and his men were forced to flee. New York City remained in British hands for the rest of the war.

The British plan for the rest of New York did not go as well. In October 1777, the British tried to defeat the colonists at Saratoga but failed. The news of the colonists' victory at the Battle of Saratoga thrilled France, Britain's enemy. The French king promised to help the colonists in their fight for freedom. In 1781, French ships helped trap Britain's main **fleet** off the coast of Virginia. Britain was finally forced to recognize the colonists' independence in 1783.

Britain was not the only loser in the American Revolution. Although New York's American Indians tried to avoid taking sides, they were forced to choose. Most fought with the British, and they paid a heavy price. In 1779, American forces killed thousands of American Indians and forced most of the rest into Canada.

In 1779, General John Sullivan and his continental troops forced New York's remaining Haudenosaunee into Canada.

NEW YORK CITY AND THE NEW NATION

In 1789, in New York City's Federal Hall, George Washington was inaugurated as this country's first president. He ran the country from there until 1790, when the government moved to Philadelphia, Pennsylvania. Over the next 50 years, New York City became the nation's most **dynamic** city. Its port was packed with ships, its **merchants** grew wealthy, and its streets had a noticeable energy.

Many people made New York City great after the revolution. One of the most important was Alexander Hamilton. Hamilton believed the government should have **authority** over the people, and control over the country's money. This increased the power of all cities, but New York City did better than any other. Hamilton also was a leader in the development of the **Constitution.**

Americans started looking west for places to settle. The best way to travel west was along New York's Mohawk River, through the Finger Lakes region, and across the Appalachian Plateau in the western part of the state. The state's population grew rapidly as people settled these **fertile** areas. Tiny villages turned into busy towns. People there needed goods and services of all kinds, and soon **upstate** New York was home to hundreds of factories. The people there felt that their opportunities were unlimited—it was an exciting time to be a New Yorker.

This building had served New York City as City Hall since 1703. It was renamed Federal Hall in 1789 and was demolished in 1812.

REGIONAL DIFFERENCES

The people in the rest of the state, however, did not always like what was happening in New York City. People

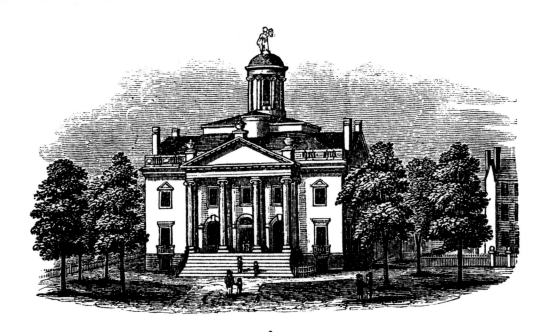

*This 1841 **engraving** shows the east view of the state capitol building in Albany.*

upstate had different lives and ideas than residents of New York City. The two groups usually voted for opposing candidates in elections. Their differences were religious, too. Upstaters were mostly Protestant, and most had been born in New York state. A steady flow of **immigrants,** however, made New York City's population increasingly Catholic and foreign-born.

Each group refused to respect the other's differences. When the people of New York City looked north, they saw simple farmers. When the people of upstate New York looked south, they saw crime and **corruption.** There was even greater conflict when the upstate city of Albany was chosen to be the state capital in 1797.

NEW INVENTIONS

The state's residents eventually found a balance that seemed to work well. The only problem was that it took too long to travel between Albany and New York City. For a few years, shipbuilders had been experimenting with steam power. Replacing a sail with an engine would make a boat faster, more dependable, and easier to move. Robert Livingston, a wealthy New Yorker, agreed to pay for a steamboat designed by Robert Fulton. In 1807, Fulton's *Clermont* chugged up the Hudson River at around five

miles per hour. It completed the trip between New York and Albany in 32 hours, and a new age of water travel was born. Using the steamboat, America's rivers—with their swift currents, tight twists and turns, and shallow waters—were soon opened to transportation and **commerce.**

Although most history books show the name of Robert Fulton's first steamboat as Clermont, *there is no historical record stating that Fulton ever used this name.*

Along with the steamboat came **ferry** service between New York's largest cities. This service brought still more people to live in New York City. Some residents began to think the city was getting too big. With so many people so close together, much could go wrong. Fire was a big threat. One spark could set dozens of houses on fire. Soon, each neighborhood had its own fire company.

Play Ball!

During the early 1800s, baseball took hold in New York City. It was first played by the members of men's social clubs. Although stories were told that said baseball was invented in the upstate village of Cooperstown in 1839, newspaper accounts dating back to the 1820s describe "base ball" games taking place in New York City. For many years, baseball and the English game of **cricket** competed for the hearts of New Yorkers. Finally, baseball won out. It became the first professional team sport in the United States in the 1870s.

Clean water was another issue for New York City. Without it, diseases could spread quickly. This problem was not solved until the 1840s, when the Croton River was **dammed** 40 miles north of the city. An **aqueduct** system was built and soon every city resident had clean water. This helped stop the spread of disease and also helped firefighters contain large fires.

THE WAR OF 1812: 1812–1814

In 1812, the United States entered into a new war against Great Britain. The United States was angry because Britain was attacking American ships and encouraging American Indians to fight against United States citizens. More than 75,000 New Yorkers fought in the War of 1812. Britain tried to control Lake Erie and

* * *

United States Naval Officer Oliver Hazard Perry is shown leaving his damaged ship, the Lawrence, *for another ship, the* Niagara. *He then continued his fight against Great Britain during the Battle of Lake Erie on September 10, 1813.*

Lake Ontario, which border New York, and Lake Champlain, within the state's borders. The United States won several victories in New York's waters, and fought the enemy near Niagara Falls.

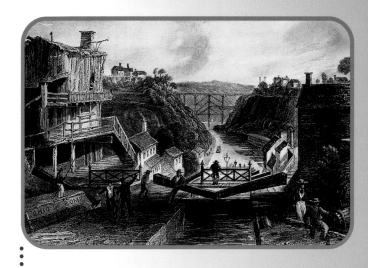

TRANSPORTATION AND THE ERIE CANAL

*This 1838 **engraving** shows a lock on the Erie Canal at Lockport, New York.*

In 1825, the Erie Canal was completed. This waterway made it possible for ships to carry goods up the Hudson River, then across the state to Lake Erie. From there, they could reach any city in the Midwest. At first, many people thought it would be impossible to build the canal. Lake Erie is 500 feet higher than the Hudson River, and getting water to "flow uphill" is difficult. Also, President James Monroe refused to pay for the project, which meant New York had to fund it. However, this turned out to be an advantage. Once the canal was built, the state did not have to share the money it made from the use of the canal with the federal government.

The Erie Canal was built in stages over eight years. A lot of the work was done by **immigrants** from Europe. A series of special **locks** made it possible for the water in the canal to rise and fall at certain points, and therefore go "up" to Lake Erie and "down" to the Hudson River. Shipping goods by water was much cheaper than sending them over land. These low prices caused a huge amount of **commerce** to flow through New York. The state grew wealthy and powerful, and New York City became the **financial** center of the nation. The Erie Canal also helped open the western United States for settlement and commerce. Farmers in the Midwest could sell their products in the east, while eastern **merchants** could sell their goods in the Midwest.

The Erie Canal

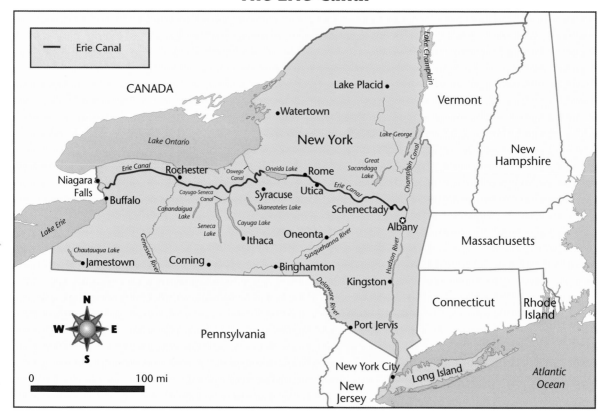

*New York **Governor** DeWitt Clinton was a very strong supporter of the Erie Canal. He saw that it would bring money to his state.*

Communities grew all along the canal. Businesses began to **flourish** in **upstate** cities. The population of Albany doubled in five years, and the cities of Buffalo, Rochester, Rome, Utica, Schenectady, and Syracuse had an explosion of **commerce** and growth. **Financiers** and **merchants** who grew rich in New York City bought huge **estates** north of the city.

The Erie Canal was enlarged in the 1830s. It remained the best way to reach the west until the 1850s, when railroads became able to compete with **barges.** The main railroad line, the New York Central Railroad, followed the route of the Erie Canal. Access lines connected to the main line ran north and south, linking the entire state. After World War II (1939–1945), a highway was also built along those lines. It connected Albany, Utica, Syracuse, Rochester, and Buffalo.

WOMEN'S RIGHTS

Unexpectedly, the Erie Canal and the new businesses it supported were a major factor in aiding the **women's movement** in the United States. So many new jobs were created that women started to work in clothing mills instead of staying home. The daughters of these women looked up to their mothers and grew up with a sense of independence. Some went off to college and realized that they did not need men to take care of them.

In most jobs at that time, women were paid only a small fraction of what men made. Those who worked in factories did so for twelve to fourteen hours per day, often in dangerous conditions. By law, a woman had to turn the money she earned over to her husband or father.

Many women thought this was not fair, and became angry. They found a leader in Elizabeth Cady Stanton, a native of Johnstown, New York. Stanton and a group of friends decided to hold a large meeting so that others could join in their fight. They placed ads in the region's newspapers. Six days later, on June 20, 1848, 300 people, including 40 men, arrived in Seneca Falls.

Elizabeth Cady Stanton addressed the first Women's Rights Convention on June 20, 1848, in Seneca Falls, New York.

The group decided that the two most important issues they believed in were women's **suffrage** and **temperance.** Women like Stanton and Rochester native Susan B. Anthony changed the way women looked, acted, and thought—and the way America treated them.

New Waves of Immigrants

The opportunities offered in New York sparked a new wave of **immigration.** In the 1840s and 1850s, as many as three million people arrived. Most were from Ireland, where potato **famines** had caused food shortages, and Germany, where a failed revolution caused many to flee.

A comparison of this 1856 view of New York with the 1651 engraving of New Amsterdam on page ten will show that the city has grown tremendously.

With so many people, so much land, and so many new ideas, New York became home to many new ideas. The **Mormon** and **Shaker** religions got their start in **upstate** New York. The Knickerbocker School of writers included Washington Irving and William Cullen Bryant. The state's natural beauty helped create the Hudson River School of painters. New York City benefited from these new ideas, too. Creative people from around the country and around the world began to move to the city. Soon it became a center of art and culture.

Slavery and the Underground Railroad

Slavery became an important issue for the people of New York. While a federal act granting the gradual **abolition** of slavery was passed in 1799, New York was

Underground Railroad Routes, c. 1860

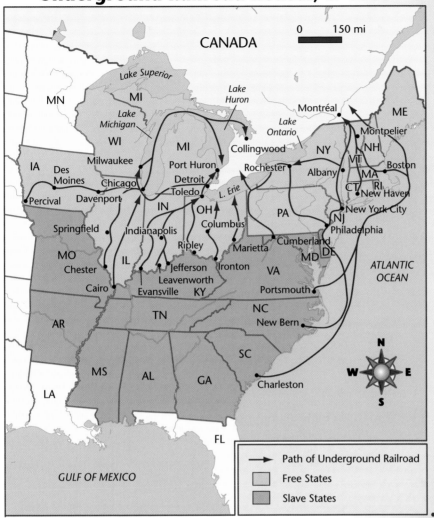

Although we will never know the exact numbers, historians estimate that in the years leading up to the Civil War, 40,000 to 100,000 slaves escaped on the Underground Railroad. Many came through New York.

one of the last northern states to legally abolish this practice in 1827. Upstate New York was at the heart of the antislavery movement. Frederick Douglass, Gerrit Smith, William Seward, and Martin Van Buren were all well-known residents involved in the fight against slavery. There were many stops for runaways in New York on the **Underground Railroad.** The state's newest immigrants, however, were not as excited about freeing the slaves. They believed that thousands of freed slaves would compete with them for their jobs.

Slavery also caused arguments in the Democratic Party, which was in control of New York state politics in the 1840s and 1850s. These arguments permitted the Republican presidential candidate, Abraham Lincoln, to win New York's votes in 1860. Unfortunately, his election divided the country and started the Civil War.

Civil War and Reconstruction: 1861-1900

The Civil War (1861–1865) affected everyone in New York. Although fighting never reached the state itself, thousands of New Yorkers were killed or wounded. New York provided 40 generals and 500,000 soldiers for the northern army. The war also encouraged business. Almost everything needed by the northern armies was made in, shipped from, or in some way paid for through New York. Despite the horrors of war, the state grew rich.

WAR PROMPTS INDUSTRY GROWTH

Because of the Civil War, New York City grew as a publishing center. Two newspapers based in the city, the *Tribune*

Draft Riots

During the Civil War, the saying "Rich man's money, poor man's blood" was often heard. It referred to the fact that rich men could pay to avoid fighting in the army. Regular men were drafted, or called to service, and had no choice but to fight. During the summer of 1863, a four-day **riot** broke out in the streets of New York City. Troops returning from the Battle of Gettysburg finally ended the fight. More than 100 New Yorkers were killed, and many more were wounded.

and *Harper's Weekly*, became important sources of wartime information. In the 1860s, many book and magazine companies established offices in the city. Libraries also grew during this time.

This 1862 Winslow Homer painting of a Civil War soldier sharpshooter was first published in Harper's Weekly.

The years after the Civil War were times of great wealth and adventure. Investors made and lost fortunes overnight, **industry** grew, and pioneers were spreading out across the west.

TAMMANY HALL

New York City **politician** William "Boss" Tweed was said to have stolen more than $200 million dollars from the city between 1866 and 1871. Tweed was the most dishonest of the Tammany Hall politicians, who were known for helping the working class and also for their dishonest business dealings. The **influence** of these politicians had been growing since the American Revolution. During the presidential races of 1828 and 1832, Tammany Hall helped Andrew Jackson get elected. Tammany was an influence in New York's Democratic Party until the 1960s.

This 1872 political cartoon by the famous artist Thomas Nast shows Boss Tweed as a powerful giant outside of the reach of the law.

The Gilded Age: 1870s

The 1870s brought important changes to New York and the rest of the nation. The United States was becoming a country based on oil, steel, machines, and railroads. This was a time when the rich and powerful could do as they pleased. This period of **prosperity** was later called "The Gilded Age." It ended in 1873, after business failures in the United States and **abroad** caused several New York banks to fail. The four-year panic that followed caused 500,000 people to lose their jobs.

New Immigrants: 1880s

In the 1880s, a new wave of **immigrants** arrived. They were mostly from Eastern and Southern Europe. From 1892 to 1911, almost all of these immigrants came through Ellis Island. Built in New York Harbor near the Statue of Liberty, it was called the "gateway to freedom."

Not everyone who came to Ellis Island was allowed to enter. Passengers were inspected by immigration officials. The officials could send them back if they were sick, or if they were thought to be criminals. Three of

Most immigrants to the United States in the late 1800s were poor, and could only afford to travel ***steerage class.***

In 1910, these Lower East Side children did their playing in a tenement alley.

every ten people were rejected for medical reasons. Because ships would not transport sick passengers back to Europe, most of the buildings on Ellis Island were hospitals. When patients were well enough to travel, they were sent back home.

Many of those who were allowed to enter settled in the **slums** of New York City's Lower East Side. They were packed into creaky wooden **tenement** houses, where unhealthy conditions and the threat of fire made day-to-day life very difficult. At one point, the Lower East Side housed 200,000 people per square mile.

Many of these new immigrants became workers in New York State's manufacturing businesses. They also did much of the labor in New York's new **industries.** During this time, working conditions were very unpleasant. Factories cared little about safety or clean air, and workers worked long hours with only one day off each week and no vacations.

New York's American Indians often worked constructing skyscrapers in Manhattan.

NEW CONSTRUCTION

By the end of the 1800s, New York City needed to solve its problem of space. From 1868 to 1875, the city's first elevator office buildings were constructed. The Equitable Life Building, Tribune Building, and Western Union Building were built on iron frames. This allowed them to be built much taller than before. If you saw them today, you would hardly think of them as skyscrapers—they were only a few stories tall. But in 1870s New York, they were the talk of the town. By the 1890s, a very strong "skeleton frame" construction allowed **architects** to design buildings a dozen stories tall. In 1913, the Woolworth Building was completed. It **dominated** the skyline at sixty stories high until the Chrysler Building and Empire State Building were finished in the 1930s.

Manhattan and Brooklyn were linked in 1883 by the city's first big architectural project, the Brooklyn Bridge. In 1898, the places surrounding Manhattan—Staten Island, Queens, Brooklyn, and the Bronx—became **boroughs** of greater New York City. This provided new land for the city's exploding population. In 1904, the city started to replace its dirty and dangerous elevated train lines with an underground subway. Within a year, many New Yorkers were traveling underground. As the 20th century began, the city had room to grow and a way to get people where they wanted to go.

This 1903 photograph shows the interior of a train car that was reserved only for women.

Modern New York: 1900–1945

New York's amazing growth continued through the early 1900s. **Immigration thrived** until the mid-1920s. Businesses grew. New York spent money on projects that helped all citizens, and passed laws to improve working conditions under Democratic **governors** Al Smith, Franklin Roosevelt, and Theodore Roosevelt.

THE TRIANGLE SHIRTWAIST COMPANY FIRE: 1911

The Triangle Shirtwaist Company was a sweatshop employing young immigrants. They were paid low wages and worked long hours under dangerous conditions.

On March 25, 1911, a fire broke out in the factory. Although there were several stairway exits, one was locked and the other was engulfed in flames. Of the 500 workers in the factory, 146 were killed. Many jumped almost 100 feet to their deaths rather than be burned alive. This tragedy resulted in the passage of groundbreaking factory safety legislation.

Firefighters tried desperately to put out the flames at the Triangle Shirtwaist Company. Their ladders could not reach the top floors.

This 1918 photograph shows children in Queens who have grown a giant cabbage in their school's war garden.

WORLD WAR I: 1914–1918

Most New Yorkers, like the majority of Americans, were at first reluctant to get involved in World War I (1914–1918). Many felt that the United States should not get involved with European affairs. But when President Wilson decided to enter the war in 1917, New Yorkers quickly showed their support. They bought **Liberty Bonds,** volunteered for the army, became members of the **Red Cross,** and worked in factories.

Something that New Yorkers of all ages did to help the war effort was work in war gardens. America's **allies** in Europe, along with American troops in Europe, needed food. The United States government began shipping tons of commercial foods to Europe. This meant there was less food for ordinary Americans. To make up for this loss, individuals, families, schools, and communities began to grow vegetables in war gardens. They then ate the food they had grown, leaving more commercial food to be shipped overseas.

THE ROARING TWENTIES

Across the nation, the 1920s were called the "Roaring Twenties." Although the sale of alcohol had been against the law since the end of World War I (1914–1918), hundreds of **speakeasies** operated in New York's largest cities. Although speakeasies existed elsewhere in the country, only in New York City did the mayor, Jimmy Walker, admit to being a regular customer.

The Harlem Renaissance

Harlem's African-American population grew dramatically during the 1920s. When the United States decided to allow fewer **immigrants** to enter the country in the early 1920s, the city found itself in need of more people to fill empty jobs. Many southern African Americans filled this need by moving north in huge numbers. In Harlem alone, the African-American population more than tripled in just a few years. This created what came to be called the Harlem Renaissance, a movement that showcased the talents of many African-American artists, musicians, poets, and authors.

But there was a dark side to the "Roaring Twenties." Criminals found that there was so much money to be made that they organized into large groups in order to control alcohol, gambling, and other **vices.** These

New York Sports Teams

In sports headlines, the Giants and Yankees baseball teams fought it out. The Dodgers baseball team also made headlines in Brooklyn. New York slugger Babe Ruth changed baseball into a power game with his home-run hitting, and Yankee Stadium became the most famous sports arena in the world. College football games drew big crowds at Yankee Stadium and the Polo Grounds, and the new National Football League was gaining fans, too. Boxing and wrestling matches were very popular, as was ice hockey. Even basketball was gaining a following, thanks to the New York Celtics.

groups paid city officials bribes, and the officials looked the other way. This led to government **corruption.** Soon, New York's "mobsters" were too large and powerful to bring down.

THE GREAT DEPRESSION: 1929

The New York Stock Exchange, founded in 1792, had become the center of the United States economy in the 1920s. When the economy crashed in the fall of 1929, the entire country went down with it. Thousands of investors were wiped out and many large companies went out of business. Millions of

This 1930s photograph shows hundreds of unemployed people waiting in line for bread during the Great Depression.

people who had never even invested in stocks found themselves penniless. New Yorkers suffered from terrible unemployment, homelessness, and **poverty.** This **era,** which lasted throughout the 1930s, was known as the Great Depression.

THE NEW YORK WORLD'S FAIR: 1939

As desperate as conditions were during the Great Depression, New York never lost its hope for the future. Much of the world shared this vision, and in 1939, countries came together in Queens to participate in a spectacular World's Fair. The theme was "Building the World of Tomorrow." The 1939 World's Fair honored the past and celebrated the future. It gave visitors a glimpse of what some people thought the future would be like.

The symbols of the fair—the Trylon and Perisphere—symbolized people's hopes and a new understanding of the world around them.

Among the highlights of the fair were **pavilions** built by different countries, as well as special exhibits showing off new technology. The hit of the fair was the General Motors "Futurama" exhibit, where visitors settled into big, soft chairs and were then moved by conveyor belt toward a **futuristic** 1960s city.

Many people who visited the RCA exhibit at the fair got their first look at something that would be in almost every home within twenty years: television. At that time, only a few hundred people in New York City had televisions.

Women in the Work Force

During World War I, many of the jobs left open by men who joined the military had been filled by women. The contributions they made in 1917 and 1918 were very important to the nation, and also convinced many women to remain in the work force after the soldiers came back home. During the 1930s, when many factories replaced workers with machines, men were fired and women were hired because they could be paid lower wages.

It was not until the United States entered World War II in 1941 that the value and abilities of female workers truly came to light. With many of the nation's young men fighting overseas and factories operating around the clock to support the war effort, there was a desperate need for workers. New York's women stepped in, and they built tanks and jeeps and guns and anything else the country needed to win the war.

Across New York, tens of thousands of women went to work and kept businesses and factories running. When the war ended in 1945, more women stayed in the work force than ever before.

Between Pearl Harbor and VJ-Day, more than three million United States soldiers made their way overseas through the Port of Embarkation in New York Harbor.

WORLD WAR II: 1939–1945

In 1941, the United States entered World War II (1939–1945). With the war came desperately needed jobs and an end to a decade of the Great Depression. The war claimed the lives of thousands of New York's young men, who went to fight overseas. It also changed the lives of many of New York's women, who went to work in the wartime factories and never left.

Once the war was won, New York was back on its feet and ready to assume an even greater role in the world.

This photograph, taken in December 1941, shows New York residents collecting scrap paper and metal. These were recycled and used to make goods needed by the United States military overseas.

Contemporary New York: 1950 to the Present

From 1950 to the present, New York has gone through many ups and downs. As the pace of life grows faster and faster, New York always looks to take the lead.

TRANSPORTATION AND THE ST. LAWRENCE SEAWAY

In the years following World War II (1939–1945), questions came up concerning the state's energy needs. The answer was clear: use the power of the Great Lakes and the St. Lawrence River. This joint effort between New York and the Canadian **province** of Ontario included the construction of power plants, as well as the deepening of shipping

St. Lawrence Seaway

— Erie Canal

— Path of ships from Atlantic Ocean to Chicago through St. Lawrence Seaway

channels. Construction began in 1954 and was completed in 1959. Today, the St. Lawrence Seaway provides miles of deep-water passage from Lake Superior to the Atlantic Ocean and serves the power needs of millions.

The years following World War II also brought dramatic changes to New York's transportation system. New Yorkers began using highways not just to travel, but to move goods from place to place. The state had improved many of its roads during the Great Depression, and during the post-war years people bought cars in record numbers. In 1954, the New York Thruway opened. It links the New York City area to Albany, Buffalo, and the state of Pennsylvania.

GROWTH OF INDUSTRY

Many felt that New York City became the world's most **influential** city during the post-war **era.** The television and music **industries thrived** in New York in the 1950s, and Madison Avenue became the heart of the advertising world. America's banking, investing, and finance industries—which influenced the global economy—were centered in New York, too. In 1948, the United Nations took up residence in a magnificent three-building complex along Manhattan's East River.

Even today, many of the country's major news programs are broadcast from New York City.

THE GROWTH OF SUBURBS: 1950s

The **prestige** and **prosperity** enjoyed by many city residents during the 1950s did not always benefit cities themselves. Families began leaving their old neighborhoods to seek a better life in other parts of the state. This "flight" to the **suburbs** harmed city neighborhoods. Local businesses closed up. In a short time, these neighborhoods became run-down. This happened not only in New York City, but in all of the state's large cities.

As wealthy residents left, mayors across the state found themselves with more city residents who needed help and fewer city residents who could pay

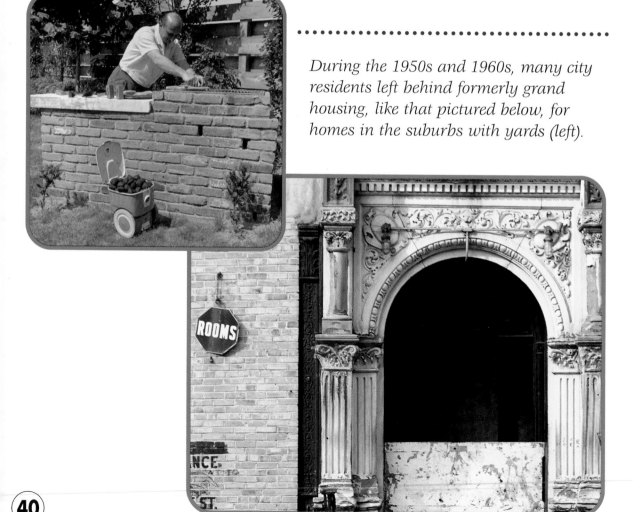

During the 1950s and 1960s, many city residents left behind formerly grand housing, like that pictured below, for homes in the suburbs with yards (left).

the taxes needed to keep their cities going. In 1958, Nelson Rockefeller was elected **governor** of New York. He served four terms, and during his time in office he added many new programs to give help to the communities that needed it. Rockefeller also expanded the state university system, offering an affordable college education to anyone who wanted one.

SHRINKING RESOURCES

Despite these programs, the problems of the cities got worse, not better. In the 1960s and 1970s, many inner cities began to fall apart. Adding to the problems of the inner cities was the fact that the number of manufacturing jobs in New York was shrinking. From the mid-1950s to the mid-1980s,

*Nelson Rockefeller was the grandson of John D. Rockefeller, an oil **industry** leader and **philanthropist**.*

600,000 of these jobs disappeared from the New York City area alone. Thousands more left other cities in the state. New York City also lost a lot of jobs at its seaport.

In 1975, New York City found itself in a horrible situation. After years of mistakes in its budget, it could not afford to pay its workers. When the city asked the federal government for help, it was refused. This forced the state of New York to pay the city's bills and invent a new way of handling money to make sure this never happened again.

In the 1940s, Love Canal, near Niagara Falls, had been used as a dump for chemical waste. Residents experienced health problems, and many were forced to move away in the 1980s.

THE ENVIRONMENT

There were problems outside New York's cities, too. For years, the government had allowed farms and factories to dispose of waste without thinking of the future. Many of New York's lakes, rivers, and streams had become **contaminated.** In some areas, the soil was poisoned with chemicals. With the air pollution of the cities added to this problem, New York was near an environmental disaster. Not until the 1960s were steps taken to fix these problems. The state's air and water are cleaner today, but there is still far to go.

THE WORLD TRADE CENTER ATTACKS: 2001

On September 11, 2001, the face of New York City was changed forever. On that day, the twin towers of the World Trade Center were destroyed by jetliners in a terrorist attack. However, New York bounced back from this horrible tragedy with characteristic grit and **resilience.** Plans are underway to create a memorial at the spot where the towers once stood, once again proclaiming the strength of New Yorkers and the American people.

Almost 3,000 people were killed on September 11, 2001, when terrorists flew planes into the World Trade Center.

NEW YORK TODAY

As we continue into the new millennium, many of New York's once-small towns are **thriving** again. New York's large cities continue to play leading roles across the country and the world. As New York peers ahead into the 21st century, it has an advantage that perhaps no other state does. Thanks to four incredible centuries in the national spotlight, it need only look to its past for the lessons it must learn to make its future bright.

Computer Revolution

Although most people think of California as the "heart" of the computer revolution, New York may have benefited even more. Every **industry** in the state gained a competitive edge due to high-speed computers and the Internet. New York's banks experienced incredible growth. Even the creative culture in New York found a new and **profitable** home in the world of computers. Thousands of the city's struggling artists and writers found steady employment, while graphic designers and "idea people" were in great demand. The result? New York experienced more widespread **prosperity** than at any other time in its history.

Map of New York

- ✪ capital
- • cities
- ∿ river
- ▓ National Forest
- ▢ National Park
- — state line

0   50 mi

Plattsburgh
Lake Champlain
Lake Placid
Adirondack Mountains
Watertown
Ticonderoga
Lake George
Lake Ontario
Oswego
Rome
Great Sacandaga Lake
Niagara Falls
Rochester
Oneida Lake
Syracuse
Utica
Mohawk River
Schenectady
Buffalo
Seneca Falls
Skaneateles Lake
Cooperstown
Albany
Lake Erie
Canandaigua Lake
Cayuga Lake
Dansville
Seneca Lake
Ithaca
Finger Lakes Nat'l Forest
Hudson
Chautauqua Lake
Genessee River
Susquehanna River
Hudson River
Binghamton
Catskill Mountains
Kingston
Poughkeepsie
White Plains
Montauk
New York City
Fire Island National Seashore

CANADA
Maine
Vermont
New Hampshire
New York
Massachusetts
Rhode Island
Connecticut
Ohio
Pennsylvania
New Jersey
Atlantic Ocean

44

Timeline

1500s	Iroquois League is created
1524	Italian explorer Giovanni da Verrazano visits New York
1609	English **navigator** Henry Hudson visits New York and claims it for the Dutch
1614	First permanent European settlement in New York, New Netherland, is settled by the Dutch
1626	Peter Minuit purchases Manhattan from the Algonquin Indians
1664	England takes control of New Netherland, and changes its name to New York
1754–1763	French and Indian War takes place; Great Britain gains control of most of New York
1776–1783	Revolutionary War is fought; many battles are fought in New York
1789	George Washington is sworn in as the nation's first president at Federal Hall in New York City
1797	Albany becomes the state capital of New York
1807	Robert Fulton's steamboat changes the way New Yorkers travel and do business
1812	New Yorkers fight the War of 1812 against Great Britain
1825	Erie Canal is completed; New York grows wealthy from shipping goods
1840–1850	Thousands of new immigrants arrive in New York, many from Ireland
1848	First Women's Rights Convention is held in Seneca Falls, New York
1861–1865	United States Civil War takes place; many New Yorkers fight for the North
1880s	New wave of immigrants arrive, mostly from Eastern and Southern Europe
1911	Triangle Shirtwaist Company fire takes place in New York City, killing 146
1914–1918	World War I takes place; many New Yorkers fight in Europe
1929	Stock market crashes; Great Depression begins. Many New Yorkers out of work
1939	New York World's Fair held in Queens; hundreds of thousands visit from all over the world
1939–1945	World War II takes place; young men fight overseas, New York's women work in factories
1959	St. Lawrence Seaway completed; Atlantic Ocean linked to Lake Superior
1950s	Cities shrink as wealthier families move to suburbs; leaders search for solutions to pay for government services
2001	Terrorists attack the World Trade Center in New York City; almost 3,000 people die in the attacks

Glossary

abolish to do away with

abroad in or to a foreign country

allies people who are on the same side during a battle or war

aqueduct structure that carries water a long distance

archaeologist person who studies history through remains of things that people have made or built

architect person who designs buildings and gives advice on their construction

artifact something created by humans for a practical purpose during a certain time period

authority power to influence the behavior of others

barge broad boat with a flat bottom used mainly in harbors and on rivers and canals

borough one of the five political divisions of New York City

commerce buying and selling goods

confederation group of people who believe in the same things and support one another

constitution written document stating the basic beliefs and laws of a nation or state

contaminate to soil, stain, or infect by contact

Continental Army American soldiers in the Revolutionary War

corruption lack of honesty

cricket English game similar to baseball

dammed having a barrier to hold back the flow of water

dominate to have a controlling position or power

dynamic full of energy

engraving art of cutting into something, especially metal, wood, or stone

era period of time starting from a specific time or event

estate large country house

famine time when food is scarce and people are starving

ferry to carry back and forth

fertile bearing crops or vegetation in abundance

financial having to do with money

financier specialist in finance, especially financing of businesses

fleet group of warships under one command

flourish to do well

frontier edge of the settled part of the country

futuristic relating to the future

governor person elected to be the head of a state of the United States; the governor is the head of the executive branch of a state government

guilder old form of Dutch money

immigrant one who moves to another country to settle

immunity resistance to a disease

industry group of businesses that offer a similar product or service

influence power of producing an effect without force or authority

Liberty Bond certificate purchased by citizens from the government during a war; the government would use the money to pay for the war, and citizens would be paid back at a later date

locks enclosure in a canal with gates at each end used in raising and lowering boats as they pass from level to level

merchant person who carries on trade especially on a large scale or with foreign countries

Mormon member of the Church of Jesus Christ of Latter-day Saints

navigator sailor responsible for sailing the ship in the correct direction

patroon Dutch landowner

pavilion building with open sides that is used for entertainment purposes

philanthropist person who gives money generously to help other people

politician person who represents others in government

poverty condition of being poor

prestige important in the eyes of many people

profitable capable of making money

prosperity succeeding in making money

province main division of a country, similar to a state

Red Cross international organization whose mission is to help those in need

redcoat member of the British Army

resilience ability to bounce back

resource something that is available to take care of a need; there are natural and manmade resources

riot outbreak of wild violence on the part of a crowd

Shaker member of a church originating in England

shellfish animal that lives in the water and has a shell

slum very poor and crowded area of a city

speakeasy place where alcoholic beverages are illegally sold

steerage class place where people paying the lowest fares stay on a ship

suburb city or town just outside a larger city

suffrage right to vote

tavern place where alcoholic beverages are sold

temperance use of little or no alcohol

tenement building separated into many small, cramped apartments

thrive to do very well

Underground Railroad system, run by people who disagreed with slavery, through which runaway slaves were secretly helped to reach freedom

upper class high position in society

upstate area north of New York City

vice wicked habit

Viking seafaring people from Scandinavia

women's movement demand for equal rights for women

More Books to Read

· ·

Elish, Dan. *New York (It's My State!).* Tarrytown, NY: Benchmark Books, 2003.

Heinrichs, Ann. *New York.* Minneapolis, Minn.: Compass Point Books, 2002.

Mattern, Joanne. *The Travels of Henry Hudson.* New York: Raintree Publishers, 2000.

Nirgiotis, Nicholas. *Erie Canal: Gateway to the West.* Danbury, Conn.: Scholastic Library Publishing, 2000.

Woog, Adam. *New York (The Thirteen Colonies).* San Diego, Calif.: Lucent Books, 2001.

Index

About the Author

Mark Stewart was born and raised in New York City and now lives across the water in New Jersey, where his office overlooks the metropolitan skyline. A graduate of Duke University with a degree in history, Stewart has authored more than 100 nonfiction titles for the school and library market. He and his wife Sarah have two daughters, Mariah and Rachel.